WHALE of DESIRE

CAT IN THE SUN PRESS

2014

WHALE of DESIRE

MICAH TOWERY

INTRODUCTION BY ALFRED CORN

Whale of Desire © Micah Towery, 2014
Introduction by Alfred Corn

ISBN: 978-0-9911523-1-5

first edition | first printing

Publisher: Joe Weil & Emily Vogel
Book design: HR Hegnauer
Typefaces: DIN, Caslon

CAT IN THE SUN PRESS
part of the REDUX CONSORTIUM

In order to be the real thing, a poet must always be a "poet in process," still searching, still developing, still testing the limits. Micah Towery is doing that, and this first collection offers us a report on the trajectory up to now. The poems in its opening pages are fantastic in the way a Chaplin silent is, with untoward or incredible events intruding on the comic plotline. Yet the narrator is more like Buster Keaton, deadpan, stoic, taking the freakish in stride as it occurs, contemplating various enigmatic assignments, for example, to "crack the moon open and pour out the glass inside." He does so with an offhand dexterity, as though he and Wyrd (in Nordic mythology, the term for "fate") were somehow indistinguishable, his actions no more controlled or predictable than the world's. In fact:

> That's how I like it, all things
> mutable, one hand outsmarting the other.
>
> ("Long Beach, Long Island")

Towery might not have been very different from other comic Surrealists like Frank O'Hara or James Tate except that atypical concerns direct the course of his development. Foremost among them is his own pilgrim's progress toward a knowledge of the divine. Nowadays such a quest most often leads the young adept to the feet of the Dalai Lama or else the writings of the Sufi mystic Rumi. In Towery's case it has led toward Christianity. Anyone suddenly losing interest should be aware that in these poems Christian ethos is presented in

concert with the oneiric, the Surreal, and even the slapstick.
Jesus is the protagonist's good buddy, his generous patron:

> After that we finished walking
> The beach's length, got some ice cream
> on the boardwalk. And Jesus picked up the tab
> like He always did back then.
>
> ("Then Jesus Turned the Camera on Himself")

"Long Beach, Long Island" announces a quest for fulfillment
in the direction of romantic love, and (as with the Jesus
poem) its setting is a seaside boardwalk. The two quests seem
related, much as we have learned to read the Song of Songs
as both a poem of erotic longing and a paean to divine love.
The same overlap is found in the Spanish devotional writers
San Juan de la Cruz and St. Teresa of Avila. In the Gospel
of John, the eternal Logos or Word is presented as light that
came into the dark world, an advent about which John says
"and the darkness comprehended it not." The Greek word
translated as "comprehended" is actually closer to meaning
"engulfed." Towery's insight is that a human response is
needed if that light is not to be swallowed up in its opposite:

> we rescue the light
> from the darkness.
>
> ("Image of a snake striking the eagle
> while being carried away")

A God that is Love must also present in human love; among the finest poems in the collection are those addressed to "Jill," the person he shares his life with. I'm not sure what to make of the fact that the love poems pull back from the Surrealist approach and seem fully credible as actions and thoughts that occurred in the real world. Is this a result of an ordering principle in the Logos, which comes to announce a new dispensation for human existence? Whatever the case, the results are moving and resonant. It's hard to think of love poems written in the past couple of decades that match the fresh, straightforward disclosures we find in these. Here is a poet who isn't afraid of saying what he feels.

I don't want, though, to give the impression that this is a stilted or inhumanly lofty book. Religion here is presented much as it is in the paintings of Stanley Spencer, something not to be separated from ordinary, civic dailiness, indeed, a spontaneous crowd of friendly folk assembling on the town green to welcome in the Good News. Also included in the volume are poems about low-level factory employment, described here with even more pungency and humor than we find in Philip Levine's portrayal of working class life. The spritz of realism and profanity recorded in "On the Closing of the Coca-Cola Plant in Binghamton, NY, Where I Worked Only Two Years of My Life (December 2008)" makes a gritty and wildly comic contrast to Towery's more metaphysical or theological poems.

In fact, one of these figures God's face as a hammer, and I'm tempted to apply the same metaphor to Towery's craft. It could be either the ball peen of an industrial worker or else a sculptor's hammer, one that overcomes the resistance of metallic or stony material. In a poem about an Egyptian sphinx viewed in an Istanbul museum, the poet takes on the imagined sculptor's voice to say:

> For this the king named me a palace sculptor.
> My rivals swung from gallows for their lack
> of vision, and my head knocked among the stars.
>
> ("First Sphinx")

With the hammer of his art, this poet has knocked on the firmament, and the firmament has opened. If the light he found there was not fully comprehended, neither was it engulfed in darkness. The light he saw, he relays to us in turn.

—ALFRED CORN

Clare Hall

The University of Cambridge

United Kingdom

02.ii.13

MEMORY IS THE
STOMACH OF THE MIND.

AUGUSTINE

Confessions, Book X

CANZIONERE 189

I wanted to be sure to reach you
—FRANK O'HARA

O ship, O battered ship
—HORACE

Like a forgetful, wind-tottered garbage scow
I float. Pity me now
I have eaten the sun god's
cattle. Hunger still grips my body.
I wanted to shield it from the gulls,
who followed the fat, dull
smell of death from port to
port, unthreading guts of trash. For you
I have been terrible, increasing,
lashed to a green whale, desiring
spontaneous prose from secret thoughts
to hold me now. Oh how sorry
I am I ate the sun's cows
and didn't feel sorry about it.

TWO DIFFERENT STORIES ABOUT
THE SAME THING, BOTH TRUE

The priests were out in Manhattan today.
They were dealing in the economics
of atonement,
they were holistic healing on buses,
chattering on Blackberries,
    catching the free fall
human spirits in their parachute cassocks.

The streets were spilled with the left-
-over vacated wine.
Woody Allen was trying to find a parking spot
for his cross.
And I was busy writing this confession
of neglect.

I was busy staring
at the naked mannequins—
not a sin, but still I'm guilty.

I asked a priest for a blessing, and
Why do good things happen to bad people?
How do I do penance for a parking ticket?
When will pigeons quit smoking—don't they know
it's bad for God's creation?

The priest said, I don't know
and I don't want to say we have only
a certain number of breaths to breathe,

but for God outside of time,
it certainly must seem that way.

.   .   .

And since it's all
make-believe anyhow,

what did St. Kevin do with his blackbird?
Because I've had several birds

try and nest on me, in my beard,
and trying to make them leave

was like catching my hand
in barbed wire...

HUNTER (SERAPH)

A tree stand waits for him
before dawn. The deer
      are still sleeping. In
darkness he rises where
perfect loneliness is.

     Now he's still
undifferentiated: unfallen
into day—though the cold will
tests him. So he enrapts him-
-self to staunch the lode

        that leaks
out in a cold brume and sags
around him, high in the tree,
where he and his body hang,
in hopes that once today

he'll spear a searching ray
      into some chest—
after which he'll lay his able back
down and rest: the first
fruits of them that sleep.

IT'S NOT THAT I DON'T LIKE CHARLTON HESTON,

that august personage
for the leading role.
Truly, Charlton Heston, you have been endowed with the
                                                    chin of God!

But Boris Karloff was given
the neck of a monster

and the chest of a wolf
    to Lon Chaney,

whose woolly idea was
to romance women
in a dry ice graveyard—

typical of such
misunderstood men,
who thought it better to steal women
than persuade them,

grow wild as the Baptist
than trim Mosaic beards
to inglorious goatees;

better to be a Roman
than a Sabine man left destitute,
when Mr. Heston came to town.

And you, O women!,
who bind me so unfairly,
who conjure up desire from thought
                    I ask,

when the moon is rising full,
and my rhetoric becomes
a guttural bark,

who among you
would rather be understood than

thrown over my shoulder
and hoisted to
the highest point in the city
with the thrilling fire of bullets
            from jealous fellows following?

NOT THERE

Sometimes at dusk
I drive a car
nobody knows I own
on a road nobody knows I drive.
(You can imagine my horror
when I see some body else I know
driving a car I don't
on the same road.
Usually, I hide behind
the wheel, and they're so busy
checking their rear view
mirror, they don't notice me.)

I look into the houses I drive by
with the lights on,
perfect in their sad
inscrutability, damp beams
through brown
lampshade blinds.
I insert my face on
the fireplace mantle,
that odd shelf—my face
into the pictures of the family,
play fetch with their old
neglected dog,
eat the leftovers in the fridge.
Nobody notices when I close the window
to the rain

or crack the moon open
and pour out the glass inside
(that's why it shines).
Nobody says thank you
when I take out the trash—it's like
I'm not even there.

POEM IN HONOR OF MY OWN BIRTHDAY

I wake up it's my birthday
and there's a fine-tuned line circling my head.
I ate breakfast across the table
from my cat.
Like *he* would tell me about that interesting article
in the Metro section this morning.
      Isn't that funny?

But what do you expect? Cats,
they read but never tell.

So what do I want
for my birthday I could tell you.
The best gift to me
was always the good weather
no more hot subway,
the last cool swig of milk
dripping down a dry throat,
or remembering the gentle moon last night
closer than you might think,
its surprising yellow,
the attractive crater scars.

I think it's clear I like
cold things, like the chilly offices
of love, the frugal re-collection
of your body
after someone's done tickling you.

It's my birthday.
I don't do what I want—
but let me say this
a little. Not too much,

and it ends
where excess should.

LOVE SONG IN THE LIGHT OF GAS STATIONS

I know that maybe comfort's being what you aren't

and being lonely is not so much about having nobody
as much as having no place when you have nobody
or your body is so limp against the sky it doesn't seem to matter.

My body has been limp in the arms of the thought of you:
             how strange this desire to sleep in a strange bed.

So instead, I've become accustomed
to false visions and vibrations,
the struggle of every little thing
and come to believe this might be a sort of love song,
a careless moment
of truth, an aloofness in which
I hear a train whistle—
I hear a church bell.

I am so impulsive for you—
I write this in the cold for you.

LATE NIGHT ARREST

I must ask how
you made me forget
my objections, my need
to get in bed early, so that I could
stay up instead and spend all night
admiring the Turkish girl with hips
I'll only describe here as "nice"—
though I think she might have been married
and perhaps I should be ashamed to admit
it did not stop me from staring. Her husband
was not around.

        Now you must already
have made love to the girl you wooed home into bed
and have fallen asleep with her head in the crook
of your arm, but I am beached, perhaps
even aloof
        and the cops are up late too.
Their lights are flashing down the street from me.
I hear them on their loudspeakers:
please step behind the police car,
        and I do,
and I think of all the women, all the Turkish girls
with admirable hips, who might just
brush their hand
        up along your side
like this cop who frisks me, asks me
where I've been, what I've had to drink.
        And I reply

that unlike you, I do not have a place
to go, even though   I do have
a cat that kneads your stomach in the morning
like a doctor searching for a hernia. And I don't have
a place where I can lay somebody's head all night,
but how happy I am
for you to be in love, my friend,
how happy.

LONG BEACH, LONG ISLAND

Somehow we ended the night on an empty
boardwalk bleacher. I'd disarmed my prejudice
against Long Island just to stand with you
and watch the lights on Fire Island flicker.

Coney Island closed that year.
The thrill of roller coasters waned
among the public. That low, eternal tone
still raked the sand from park to bleacher.
My right hand held yours

or wanted to. But one hand didn't know
what the other was doing, and my left
kept murdering you in turbid surf.
That's how I like it, all things
mutable, one hand outsmarting the other.

MOTH (PSALM 39)

Wanting to avoid your violent side, I tried to keep
my mouth shut when I saw the way you
rigged this game to destroy beauty—

and not just beauty, but the gaudy,
fast food smut I hoard, too—
savored by the hungry

moth. But you always hated the grudging
"Yes" and made me broach the issue
of how you snatch away another's beauty

in gloating silence, leave us bleached,
belly-up whales on the sand's ecru:
Not even a bone to gnaw at when I'm hungry?

It's either you or *vanity, vanity...*
So yes, you have my yes. And true,
this might have been the point: your beauty

is a bitter sponge of lye you lift up daily
to my mouth, while you consume
me with the blows of your hand—my beauty,
a moth, feeding, still hungry.

PROLOGUE

In the beginning was the Word
        and the Word was a hammer
        and out of nothing the hammer banged
something: a hippo, a peach, a lightbulb.

           And the hammer was the face of God
—not a metaphor—the hammer was God,
              and this sort of responsibility didn't faze Him.

When it was time to make man, the hammer decided
        to sleep on it, woke up very early
           the next morning under the turning
           of the sixth sun, picked himself up and

from the afterbirth of creation, he formed man

to be like Himself, so that man would not be found
        faceless, void.

        And when man first opened his eyes, saw
           the hammer like a child looks at its mother,
              certainly man loved the hammer for giving life.

        But man tired
      seeing his own face in the face of the hammer, when he met
      the hammer in the cool of the morning,
        every morning,

so man found the nearest mirror, and in
what was supposed to be
a point of great irony, plunged his face into it.

Later, when the hammer
came back to fix things,
it became
a hammer.

THE HOLY SPIRIT AT THE BAPTISM
OF CHRIST

*...the Spirit of God descending
like a dove and lighting on Him...*
— MATTHEW 3:16

More akin
to a falling mirror
of a dove
than the dove itself—

flat as a page
with depth
and that deepness turning itself
in many dimensions,

somehow expanding
finitude, a black hole
of light—
this must be where gravity goes—

this is how God answers
His own prayer:

the voice of God
conforms itself to a whisper—

the whisper submits
to the wind, blown
this way, that—

what happened over
the waters of creation
broods again
over new waters.

FROM THE ISTANBUL ARCHEOLOGY MUSEUM

1. ### Curse on grave robbers
    from a grave stele

    May a pack of seven wild
    and particularly
    mangy dogs
    find your stone
    and carry away your
    bones by the ankles.

    And if this is not enough,
    you will also pay
    a fine of 500 denarii
    to the city for the crime
    of grave robbery.

2. First Sphinx

This was the first of many sphinxes
I made of the king. I crafted his chest
as locust armor, evidence of his all-consuming wrath.
In contrast were the wings, which I modeled after palm
to show his kindness as a shade to those
who paid the tribute of friendship.

These days there is unseen wisdom in this sphinx's
manner, an accident I would have thought
an imperfection when I made it: how his chest
seems also like a hive of honey, how the wings
sway like fire through alien wheat.

But one thing stays unchanged by time
and patient observation. For it
the king applauded, and I silenced skeptics
of my skill: hung between his lion legs—of this
no doubt—swing the true balls of a King.

For this the king named me a palace sculptor.
My rivals swung from gallows for their lack
of vision, and my head knocked among the stars.

3. Image of a snake striking the eagle while being carried away

from a Manichean temple

This image has no mother.
It was found in a river
by a ferryman whose boat
was overturned
by fierce winds.
    As he sank
down to the bottom
he saw this snake—
not eating its own tail as
many had supposed. Instead
he saw that it was striking
at the eagle carrying it off
to be eaten.

The ferryman decided
then that it was not
a good day to die, so he swam
to the shore with this image
carved in stone.

Now we use it
as a place to offer
incense. In this way
we rescue the light
from the darkness.

AN INVITATION (HORACE'S ODE I.20)

Cheap wine, Maecenas! You'll drink cheap wine from cheap cups,
our local Sabine swill. I pitched the Grecian jar myself, and filled
                                    it with wine

I,made. I laid it in my cellar on that day you entered your theater
after a long sickness. Yes, Maecenas, the people saw you and cheered

and the echoes filled Rome, your Tiber trembled and the Vatican
                                 hills shook. Yes,
Maecenas, it's true—you've drunk the crushed grapes of Calenia
                                 and Caecuba.

You've had Falernia and Formia—better wine than my cups
                                 should ever dirty.

FISHING AT RANDOM IN THE STREAM OF MY HEART

To-do lists stretch out my door while
I spoon coconut milk from a can
with my finger. This milk's full
sweetness puts it to a list I keep
but don't write down—things
of self-evident goodness: like honey,
coffee slick with oils, eggs cooked in butter
in my grandmother's cast iron skillet.

.   .   .

Chuang Tzu says it's good to float
on the river as an empty boat, since
even bad men don't get angry when
an empty boat bumps into them,
and I am, in a certain way, empty, but
my boat keeps catching in familiar
currents. It pushes back into the same
bank of reeds without even
a rudder movement from me.

THEN JESUS TURNED THE CAMERA
ON HIMSELF

Thomas was insistent we get one
by the seaside, since the sun was so nice that day
on the water. And after some attempts with a timer
snapped Thomas, blurred, running deeper into frame
towards us, laughing, beckoning him, *run faster!*,
Jesus volunteered. We all thought
it turned out nicely, if I remember.

Then Jesus turned the camera on Himself
and made a funny face, but His holiness
broke the camera. Must've happened when
the camera tried to take the glare out of
his eyes. Anyways, we stared, not sure
what to say. Thomas looked pissed. But Jesus
was never one to let a friend down.

He kneeled low in the dirt, mixed spit and dust.
Then rubbed it on the lens—Thomas
almost had a heart attack. (This was before
the time Peter got drunk at that wedding
in Cana and me and Jesus carried him
home to his wife on our shoulders.)

Jesus gave the camera back to Thomas,
mumbled about making all things
new, and Thomas used to say from that point on
his camera took the oddest pictures, like angels
dancing on the heads of pins and flaming chariots
swooping down to ferry the supremely faithful
to Heaven—but who could believe him?

After that we finished walking
the beach's length, got some ice cream
on the boardwalk. And Jesus picked up the tab
like He always did back then.

SAD SAINT AUGUSTINE

You're in the Neoplatonic backseat,
so to speak, with that beard
you've been trying to grow for weeks.

You lean back in your chair, glum tabby
in arm because he teaches you
to worship God in the
warm sunlight from the window.
He bats your hair, knocks loose
a halo of dust around your head
in the afternoon dusk.

I like to listen sometimes
when you take out your steel guitar
and slide your sorrow into the strings.

Is that a hymn?

I like the sound you make
when you hum to yourself.

The teapot whistles,
and I smell the cigarette
you smoke over your thoughts,
stroking your pious bald spot.

Downstairs, I can hear everything,
your sweat hitting the floor,
the cries and moans
of cities, invisible.

TRIBUTE TO HERMAN MELVILLE

You are a leather-bound apocalypse
each account a jazz piece—
   you solo up and down the pages.
So to get a better grip
   I hammer them to the floor like gold doubloons
   and walk upon your words as Christ
   walked upon the sea.
But you warned me
   that the truth can shake a man.
Only you can tell me about
   this empire, the transfiguration
   of whales mating in the deep.

You leviathan—
laughing at the children who are laughing at you.
You're taking out my brain and smoking it again
   like the cheap, cherry-flavored cigar it is.
My hairs are splitting you—

You drunk—
I don't think Hawthorne will ever return your calls
   to comfort your disconsolate
   and Goliath ways.
Don't sit there like a kid whose dad never plays catch.
Pick up your cosmic phone
   and call me again.
Take out your electric guitar
   and riff, riff, riff.

MILES DAVIS LIVES IN MY CLOSET

Miles Davis lives in my closet.
Sometimes he comes out to play for me.
And sometimes he stays in there alone,
          and I hear his blues
muted by my hanging clothes.

Coltrane plays to help me fall asleep.
He sits under my bunk bed
and his saxophone echoes on the empty summer streets
          through my open window.

T.S. Eliot comes over.
He gives me advice on women
and reads his latest poetry at my kitchen table.
Is it about being sad? I ask him,
          and he sighs
while Miles and John
play together upstairs.

I LEAVE HIM THERE

after and with lines from Michael S. Harper

From your head's darkening,
where brass tunnels play,
it meets you,
a fond memory founds you,
Gnostic labels finally escape you
and accidentally
you find...

smacked out on
modes, I'd almost forgotten
my suspension
on the pentatonic scale. Miles
of useless vocabulary
fall off
the average tongue, but
what else you gonna play with?
Diatonic lacerations
whipping the ear,
flashing slowly in the night.
It bleeds until...

it begins to sing
from your uncle's sap farm—
fifty gallons maple sap
to make a gallon of maple syrup and this
is appropriate:
you boil forever, but
a minute too long,
it's ruined.

Now sing
threnody: the lost
graces,
I Remember Clifford
the last night he played in Philly,
dead at 25
on the Pennsylvania Turnpike
west of Bedford, and I
have not even begun:

You play only in vowels!
Thank you God.
You think you make
the world spin round
Thank you God.
with air?
Thank you God
for the air
for the trees
*for the birds and bees…*And then

dawn in the Parlor City,
foot rest of the dying Electric City,
I listen on broken headphones
on the bus: cold
ar   peggio mix-
-olydian flat   E ^{sus}
^{9}: I tap finger window
and you offer yourself
up, sacramental,
almost paschal.

A friend told me
Christ is risen
above jazz—
I leave Him there.

ON THE CLOSING OF THE COCA-COLA PLANT IN BINGHAMTON, NY, WHERE I WORKED ONLY TWO YEARS OF MY LIFE (DECEMBER 2008)

> "How do you train a horse?"
>
> "Which horse?"

I. Invocation

Goddammit Gatto you perv
your Mack truck porn
stash Ed my boss
and his boss Jeff
Ziggy Little John Big John the guy
who never washed his hands after taking
a shit mechanics drivers sideloaders
still running at three hundred thousand miles—God-
damn you Union go fuck yourself.

Praise you, laid off workers, part timers,
injured and summer laborers like me
who got out.

Goddamn the rest of you—

I know you had no place to go...

II. Summer Labor

Sometimes Charlie shovels soda shit
and dust that has collected
in the drainage pit, mixed
with tobacco juice.

The whole plant smells for weeks
after he mucks it,
but Charlie likes to do it—
warehouse couldn't take the farm boy out

of him even though his brother,
Big John, lost it long ago.
In the break room,
where we get our routes, I

am the bottom of the totem
pole, the mouth that eats
the shit that rolls downhill
always. Here's a flowchart

like we got in meetings:
Corporate—>Salesmen—>
Union—>Drivers—>
Summer Labor. Ziggy pimps

the worst routes onto me. *Sorry, kid.*
After the break room,
we walk into the yard
of broken skids and empties,

vacant Coke machines. Shop steward
Mike waits on his forklift
impatient to finish
the same work he does

every day. Dennis,
the warehouse idiot,
spins in the yard out of
sheer boredom, his forklift.

The hottest mornings of summer
we get here early. It's
still. Summer dark
fogs the windshields

and these men, left behind—
only a matter of time
until Binghamton plant closes
and we all become Crowley

Milk men, who have the same
but better union, who taunt me
in the backs of supermarkets:
You Coke guys eat more shit

than my dog.
I put product on the shelf
and declare, I am only
here for summer.

III. Your Father in the Early Morning

To mine

You and your dad also delivered soda:
RC—Pepsi—Coca-Cola—

three carbonated mortal enemies.
Which brand does our lineage bleed?

Sometimes I think your father
(in the early morning—his godlike

absence from your mother's side)
pulled his car onto the gravel bed that day

just to shoot at birds. I would've
thought that made you sad enough.

But still there is no smell more potent than
your breath and sweater pressed
        against my face.

IV. A Psalm for Ralphy

Of all the men I feel sorry for
most, there's Ralphy,

who lost his wife
after thirty years—

The end of marriage
is a death, he told me,
but I was dead
for years, a slug.
This job will kill you.

Three years ago she left him.
The other men remember her
the way they did
when Ralphy came in
and was sent home drunk
three days straight—*cunt,*
        bitch.

            Canned spaghetti and chewing tobacco—two Cokes
                    and a cigarette for lunch.

Ralph lost his house
to the flood that closed the plant three days.
        I miss my sandwich iron most, he said.

V. Ubi Sunt

All I have to ask
is what
happens to Ed, my old boss?

Almost to retirement
anyway,
but what'll he do now

with all that free time—only so many
Yankee games
on TV—only so much retirement to gamble away.

Can he know his wife again?
Can she
forgive him for playing softball

on their wedding day?
And Curtis—
you know that this job saved his life

when the cancer and his wife were taking
the last
of what he had. Did you know

the Wal-Mart cola section was his pride? His reason
to shower
every morning? Where will he sleep now? In what

company car? Who remembers now
the useless
knowledge the old guys taught us: how to

sweet talk the gas station ladies—
how to
get free donuts and coffee—

how to calm ghosts
in the limbo
of convenience store coolers?

AT GARY'S U-PULL IT

Nothing's guaranteed at GARY'S
U-PULL IT: only the rust, sun,
and rubber refuse time. No metal
can last. When the snow melts,

the junk sinks faster into mud.
Here miracles are brand new
tires still attached to smithereened
windshields, hoods unlatched

and twisted beyond the manufacturer's
dimensions. Here all succumbs
to a forlorn man with a wrench
and socket set. He stands waist-deep

in the ever frozen river
of wrecked metal and roots
for a coolant reservoir to rig
his car with. At GARY'S U-PULL IT

no one laughs at "Shit happens"
on the bumper of a car
with a caved roof, and the "A+
Honors Student" is probably a prick

who gets his shit kicked
at school. Here all hungers—
here desires: here I pit an unclaimed
tire iron against a windshield

when nobody looks anymore or asks
in passing who this air-bag exploded for.

IN WHICH WE PRAY THE PRAYERS
OF EUCHARISTIC ADORATION

We eat too much—
too many fries
        and fried food.
We barely walk
And smoke no
        cigarettes
because Joe quit
last May. And
since we cannot
        talk on such
        full stomachs,
we have no choice
        but prayer.

The Leroy Street church
        has a chapel
        just for Eucharistic
adoration.
        We ask
one miracle: to walk
and not be sore.

What whales
          have swallowed us?
Spit us up and beached us
          on these pews?
Two gluttons
          who pray
in a baptism
          of sweat,
gazing, unable
          to partake,
even if we could
          reach the rail
and kneel.

How many times
          the Rosary?
How many vigils
          and midnights
          pass before
          they throw us out?

But may they find us
          too heavy—

May they leave us
          to our ways—

May we become
          two fattened saints
stupid with prayer.

AN AUTISTIC CHILD SWIMS WITH DOLPHINS

I am more free, chained
eloquently, bound and
pressed against—
this water and this dolphin.
My first movements were confession—
My thoughts a hidden syntax—

even in the womb I spoke, numb
I spoke, dumb I spoke. I was knit
in surprise. My spine was twisted
but it was restored—therefore
my cradle was made of bone
and I lacked no body for speech.

I counterpoint even hands to fingers,
choose instead, no word for sorrow.

FIRST LOVE POEM FOR JILL

after 3 years

Maybe it was the nervousness
        I learned from my father
that made me such an ass sometimes,
        made me smirk each time you'd say,
"I'm glad I have you." Such disquiet
        won't attribute acts of man to God,

yet must divine in them
        a plan, and in that work I never rest
at the conveyor belt of facts
        and circumstance (this, you noted well,
makes a relationship with the sublime

        complex). Even now I struggle
with the happenstance that made us one,
        with the gelid light you pointed to in awe
when it fell on Mt. Baker: somehow I've felt
        it was not equal to the ease,
the worldless sense of "Our Prayer/Gee",
        which I want and fear. So thus far

I've left it—unspoken, mouth-shut,
        like the Psalmist in reverse,
lest incantation have the opposite effect
        and unmake, the shade recede
into the unformed wake, waved back
        by the hand of my agitated heart,
back into the storehouse of my memory.

But now I see that I am Saul at Endor,
          deprived of a prophet, gnarled in
and small like a toenail—that I seek
          any awkward go-between which leaves
the veil in place because I fear what might
          come real if I call out
from my valley of my shadow. Please

          forgive my tedious *coeur*,
true love; it feels but doesn't know
          beauty begins terror.
It hasn't learned to fall yet
          into the vertigo of gratitude.

SECOND LOVE POEM FOR JILL

In Idaho

Down at the boat launch, on the river that feeds
        into Lake Pend Oreille,
the slanted concrete slab still warmed us where
we sat, and the mountains faded into the sky
        as the train went by
        to Coeur D'Alene.

I stared into the clear and moving water
        at the rocks
until I saw how full the water was of fish—so full—
such was the light—after a while I saw only
        the fish after the rumble
        passed away.

On that evening when we'd spent the day
        negotiating, careful,
you said to me, *I'm figuring out marriage
and you and figuring out me*, and the river
        in its wisdom
        said nothing wise.

And the water glinted with the last light of the bugs
        that broke
the surface, and it sounded with the fish that ate them.
And the mountains kept fading into the sky.
        Then you said,
        I love...

and didn't finish. So we left the launch
      and drove
away, and the river echoed that *I love*. And
afterwards, a moose began to wade across
      the water
      slowly.

THIRD LOVE POEM FOR JILL

Now I have you, here
      in the full sweetness
of the moment: when you prepare
      your advent calendar, as you do
each year, underneath an advent
      wreath you've hung already
in our window, red and
      white and green, made to misdirect
the wisemen and the shepherds
      until you're ready
for His coming once again.

Almost—as I view you
      from the kitchen—I almost
come behind to hold you. And later,
      after dinner, I am full of sadness that
I didn't. And I'm sad the roast
      I labored over lies half-eaten,
leaking on the cutting board.
      And you no longer stand
at the dining room table,
      cutting and tying cloth
to a hanger, framed against
      the early evening darkness.

And when these things are also gone,
        and I wash dishes at the sink, I am
breathtaken that there was a time
        which isn't anymore.
There was a vivid life I had,
        and now I have another.
This fills me with fear and wonder,
        how one realness
piles one upon the other.

How easily the lie of time
        betrays us, and we think
that all things pass outside our
        selves, when in fact
it's we who pass away
        in our distention.

And tomorrow, I forget this all again
        as I drink my coffee and, the next day,
will forget that too—until I
        gasp with awe at some bright smell
or sound that brings you, now,
        the wreath and advent calendar, back.

Jill, Jill—I use your name
        again, I turn it in my head
and mouth, that by which I call
        and curse and yet
still know you, the whiteness of
        your name, of you to me,
unchanged, as a stone.

NEW YEAR'S

The landlords laugh
      in Catonese
upstairs. They blow their noses
      late into the night.

Downstairs, I sit
      in a haiku
almost. Snow crusted
      on the neighbor's roof.

The forest behind
      the house resembles
a sea of stiff reeds. The sky
      sends down enough glow

to write by. Jill's
      red wreath still hangs,
dark, in the window. I'd like
      to be the wine

we're aging in the cool
      bedroom, sealed
and developing in secret:
      mute, the changes,

trivial almost, from one
      day to the next. When I turn
the electric baseboard
      heaters to low,

a dingy hue sinks
        into the dark living room. Now
the restless birds settle
        in the eaves. And now Jill

opens and closes
        books in the study.
I think myself without desire,
        but the sound of cars

outside, the automatic fan
        in the bathroom, low
rumble of the central heat,
        each house's own

industrial furnace. And
        I see now no Tang
poet would recognize
        the unnatural radiance

of the sky (from nearby
        greenhouses), the high
pitch of engines gunning up
        our hill. Even

the Zodiac, marching
        over us again,
seems out of sight.
        The words I find for this

have been heard before—
        but who
will see what is here
        if I do not:

the house crusted with snow
        the forest like stiff reeds?

BRYAN

Bryan, the dishwasher, keeps me company,
late night on the bus. When I have not yet
driven into the early morning, he
is riding home to his empty apartment,
to reheat dinner before crashing
into bed. Bryan tells me the same jokes
with the same stories in between—
how he used to be an engineer's apprentice—
the time he and the other men had to rebuild
eighty feet of rail track in the yard when
an engine plowed through too fast and it was
ten degrees below. "That was the coldest
I'll ever be, I know it," he tells me.

Sometimes he looks out the window when we pass
the big pink Catholic church on Conklin,
and talks about the summer dusk on that
great Tioga line, about that time of day
when kids stop throwing rocks at boxcars
and run home instead: in the distance you hear
church bells echo through the mountains
or another train whistle somewhere far off.
He used to fall asleep to the summer air
through his hat and smell of fish cooked from
the river when he should've watched the tracks.

I ask if he ever heard Shakespeare
in the endless iamb click-clack of the rails
beneath the speeding engine, or if
Kerouac ever hopped a ride to put him
to sleep with his blues, or if the engineer
ever caught him napping like a hobo.

We pass the Skylark Diner—I ask again
how he got away with it, how he was never
caught dozing to the railroad's metal sonnet,
or how he dealt with the frostbite I know
he had from the way he rubs his hands when
the bus gets cold. I know Bryan tells me
everything with enough late night bus rides.
He will let me in on everything.

I know these stories. Jesus, he's told me
a hundred times. And I know his time is short
because he's said so. Last night he saw a cop
prod a sleeping bum with a nightstick
and said, "I know that's my lot soon. God,
I'm not here long." But I don't think about it.
I don't hear his empty cough rake through the bus—
not now—because now we're lifting high upon
the arch of the Chenango Street bridge, almost
to his apartment, almost over the old
and abandoned rail lines.

MORNING SONG

after Galway Kinnell

Then it was morning in wintertime.
I boiled some water, peeled a potato.
The radiator clanged and whistled its sorrow.
Now was the best time for solitude.
The milk man whistled his sorrowful tune
of New York mornings in wintertime.

I filled the cat's bowl as he was still yawning.
The hot water begun to beat its rhythm
against the shower curtain. Steam
curled underneath the bathroom door.
I put the cat's food bowl on the kitchen floor
and broke an icicle sprung from the awning.

In the fog, the light of dawn hung,
steadfast, above the frost-rimed ground.
Everything was lost in its music, or found.
I seasoned the pan with two broken eggs
and listened to a car pass through the fog:
the sound of morning as its sorrow was sung.

ON THE REFRAIN TAKEN FROM
AN OLD HYMN

Be still, my soul,
      by the radiator.
Be still the way a noisy phone line is to fish
      along the ocean floor.

Be still, impatiens quickly blooming.

Be still when breaking shafts of light
      in a musty old brain of an attic
      cleaning away the cobwebbed dust.

Be still, my soul,
      like a math equation.
Be still, my soul,
      like condensation on a beer glass.
The way the feathers of a feather are when it's blown,
      still, be still, my soul.

Like my father deep in reading contemplation
      or when napping
or thick stained glass, long after the service
      has ended.
The way my mother draws blood from her patients.
The way my brothers were in love with girls in middle school.
Be still.

Be still the way creation was before it was created

before it sang with the morning stars.

NOTES

"CANZIONERE 189"

This poem is a rehearsal of Wyatt's "My galley charged with forgetfulness," a poem based on Petrarch's loose rendition of Ode i.14 by Horace. The line from Frank O'Hara comes from his own 'translation' of Wyatt/Petrarch/Horace.

"TWO STORIES ABOUT THE SAME THING, BOTH TRUE"

The Woody Allen movie referenced is *Bananas*.

"I LEAVE HIM THERE"

The Harper poem referenced is "Alone" from *Dear John, Dear Coltrane*: "A friend told me / He'd risen above jazz / I leave him there." The Parlor City is Binghamton, NY. The Electric City is Scranton, PA.

"AN AUTISTIC CHILD SWIMS WITH DOLPHINS"

Dolphin Assisted Therapy is a sometimes used for autism.

"MORNING SONG"

This poem loosely follows the rhyme scheme from Galway Kinnell's poem "First Song" from *What a Kingdom It Was*.

ACKNOWLEDGMENTS

Big Hammer: "On the Closing of the Coca-Cola Plant in Binghamton, NY, Where I Worked Only Two Years of My Life (December 2008)"

Blue Fifth Review: "Brooklyn Tenebrae"

Cimarron Review: "New Year's"

Circus Book: "Another Prayer and Love Song"

Drunken Koudou: "Sad Saint Augustine"

Gulf Stream: "Three Visions of Great Grandfather with a Knife"

Paterson Literary Review: "On the Refrain Taken from an Old Hymn"

Prime Number Magazine: "At GARY'S U-PULL IT"

Pyrta: "Canzionere 189," "I Leave Him There"

Ragazine.cc: "The Holy Spirit at the Baptism of Christ," "Tribute to Herman Melville"

[spaces]: "Long Beach, Long Island," "The Prologue of John"

This Great Society: "Two Different Stories about the Same Thing, Both True," "Feeling Like Shit in Binghamton," "Love Song in the Light of Gas Stations," "Late Night Arrest"

THANKS

My wife and partner, Jill. My family. Joe Weil, *consigliere*, friend and teacher, and his beautiful family—Emily, Clare, Gabriel. Tom Sleigh, for his generosity. Alfred Corn, for his friendship. Everyone from THEthe Poetry Blog, especially Stewart, Adam, Lisa, Gene. Everyone from Hunter, especially Donna Masini and Jan Heller Levi, Colie and Chris. Everyone who let me couch surf in NYC. Everyone I crossed paths with in Binghamton: Maria Gillan, Christine Gelineau, Sean Thomas Dougherty, Sue Ellen Thompson, Adam, Joel, Eric, Flo, Brian, Metta, Racquel, Jeff, Tom, Dana, Jessica, Jan, Hillary, the poor bastards from the Coke plant. Friends from Good Shepherd (Matt and Anne), CTR, and St. Augustine's. Friends and mentors from TWU, ESLI, IUSB, and Ivy Tech. Josh and Cassandra, Travis and Katie, David and Carol, Brooks and Dana, Steven. Everyone else from the Den of Sin.

BIO

Micah Towery studied at Binghamton University and Hunter College. He teaches and helps run thethepoetry.com.

24771212R00043

Made in the USA
Charleston, SC
07 December 2013